LIFE SERIES

A Time to Play

Level 2
Seventh-day Adventist Readers

Patricia A. Habada

Anna Dunbebin

Sally J. McMillan

Mitzi J. Smith

Bill   Ted   Nan   Jill   Ben   Lad   Rosa

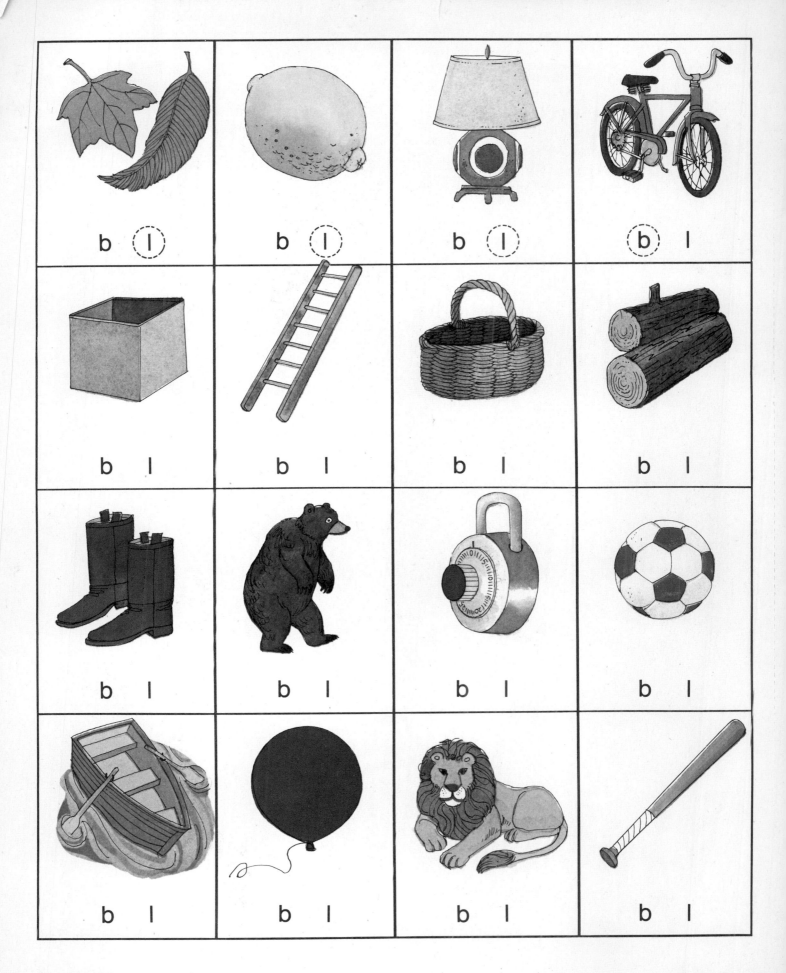

b (l)   b (l)   b (l)   (b) l

b l   b l   b l   b l

b l   b l   b l   b l

b l   b l   b l   b l

Bill   Bill   Bill

Bill

Bill   ill

Bill

Bill

Bill

Bill

Lad   Lad   Lad

Lad

Lad   ad

Bill   Lad

Bill   Lad

Lad   Bill

Lad   Bill

Bill runs.

Lad runs.

runs   runs

Bill runs. —————————

Lad runs. —————————

Lad runs. —————————

Bill runs. —————————

Bill hides.

Lad hides.

Bill runs.

Bill hides.

Lad runs.

Lad hides.

Lad runs.

Lad hides.

Bill runs.

Bill hides.

Decoding: /b/<u>b</u>, /l/<u>l</u>, /r/<u>r</u>, /h/<u>h</u>

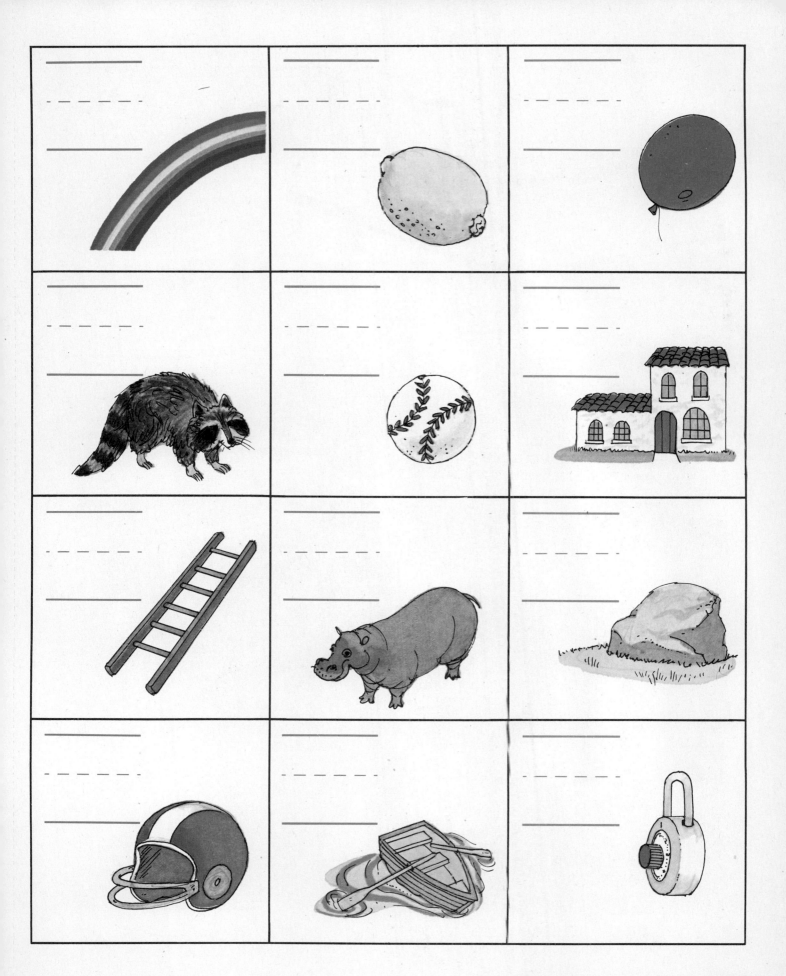

Row 1:
(j) b l   j b (l)   (j) b l   (j) b l

Row 2:
j r h   j r h   j r h   j r h

Row 3:
j b l   j b l   j b l   j b l

Row 4:
j r h   j r h   j r h   j r h

Jill   Jill   Jill

Jill

Jill   ill

Bill hides.

Jill hides.

Bill runs.

Jill runs.

Lad runs.

Jill runs.

Lad runs.

Jill runs.

and   and   and

Bill and Jill

and   and   _____

●   ● Jill and Bill

●   ● Lad and Bill

●   ● Jill and Lad

Go   Go   _ _

Go, Jill, go.

go   go   _ _

Jill and Bill go.

Jill hides and Bill hides.

Jill runs and Bill runs.

Jill and Bill go.

Go, Jill.

Jill hides.

Bill and Jill go.

Jill hides.

I am I am

I am Jill.   I am Bill.

I am

I am Jill.

Jill hides.

Jill and Bill go.

I am Jill.

Bill runs.

I am Bill.

Lad and Bill go.

I am Bill.

I am Rosa.

Rosa ___osa ___ ___

I am Rosa.

I am Lad.

Rosa runs.

Bill runs.

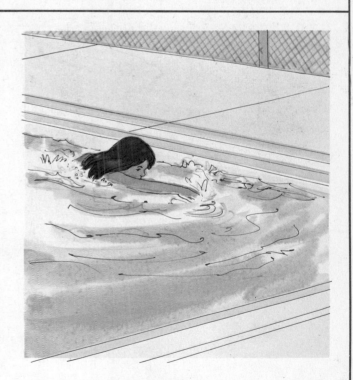

Lad and Rosa go.

Rosa and Jill go.

Go, Rosa, go.

Go, Bill, go.

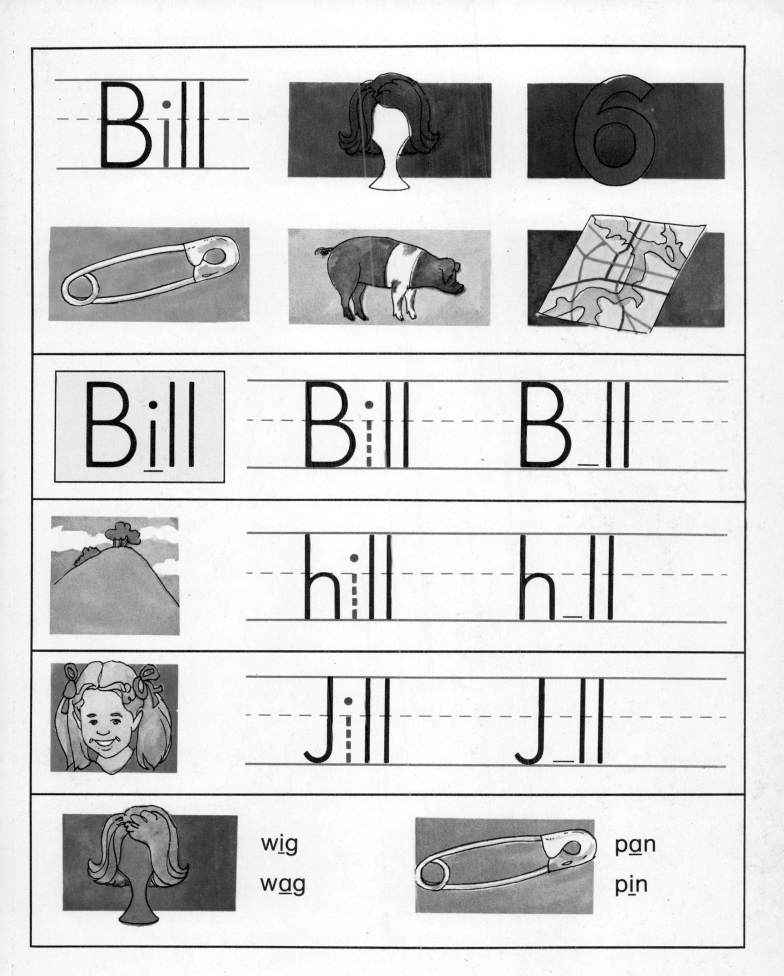

Bill

Bill Bill B_ll

hill h_ll

Jill J_ll

wig
wag

pan
pin

j b (c)	j (b) c	j b (c)	(j) b c
l c j	l c j	l c j	l c j
c j r	c j r	c j r	c j r
h j c	h j c	h j c	h j c

rides   rides   rides

Bill rides.

Jill rides.

rides   rides

Bill hides.

Bill runs.

Bill rides.

Jill rides.

Jill runs.

Jill hides.

Lad rides.

Lad hides.

Lad runs.

Lad hides.

Lad rides.

Lad runs.

Rosa and Jill ride.

Lad runs.

ride _ide _ _ _

Rosa and Jill run.

Lad rides.

run _un _ _ _

Rosa and Lad hide.

Jill runs.

hide _ide _ _ _

Jill and Rosa ride.

Jill and Rosa run.

Jill and Rosa hide.

Bill and Jill ride.

Bill and Jill hide.

Bill and Jill run.

Jill and Bill hide.

Jill and Bill run.

Lad runs.

Lad hides.

Jill and Bill hide.

Lad and Bill run.

Can Jill ride?

Jill can ride.

can ___an ___ __

Can Rosa and Jill ride?

Rosa and Jill can run.

Rosa and Jill can ride.

Rosa and Jill can hide.

Can Lad hide?

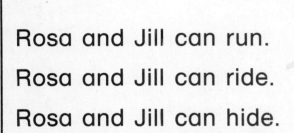

Lad can ride.

Lad runs.

Lad can hide.

Can Jill run?

Jill can run.

Jill can ride.

Jill hides.

Rosa can ride this.

Lad can hide this.

Can Jill ride this?

Jill hides this.

Jill can ride this.

Jill can run.

Can Rosa ride this?

Rosa can ride this.

Rosa can hide this.

Rosa can run this.

Can Bill and Jill hide this?

Bill and Jill go.

Bill and Jill hide this.

Bill and Jill ride this.

ZOO PONY RIDES

Can Bill Ride?

Can Bill ride this?

Bill rides this.

Lad runs.

Can Bill ride?

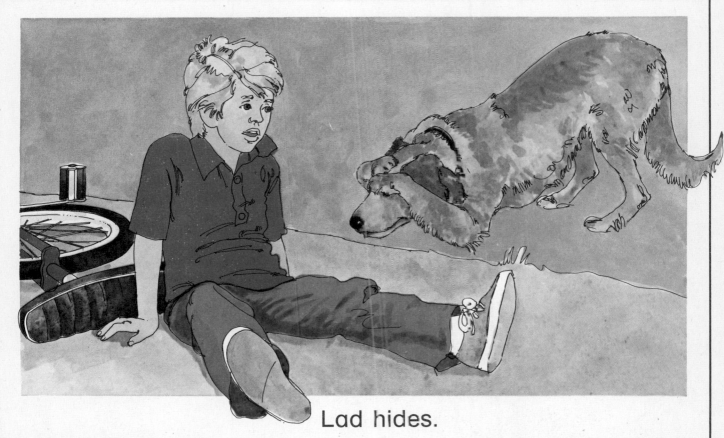

Lad hides.

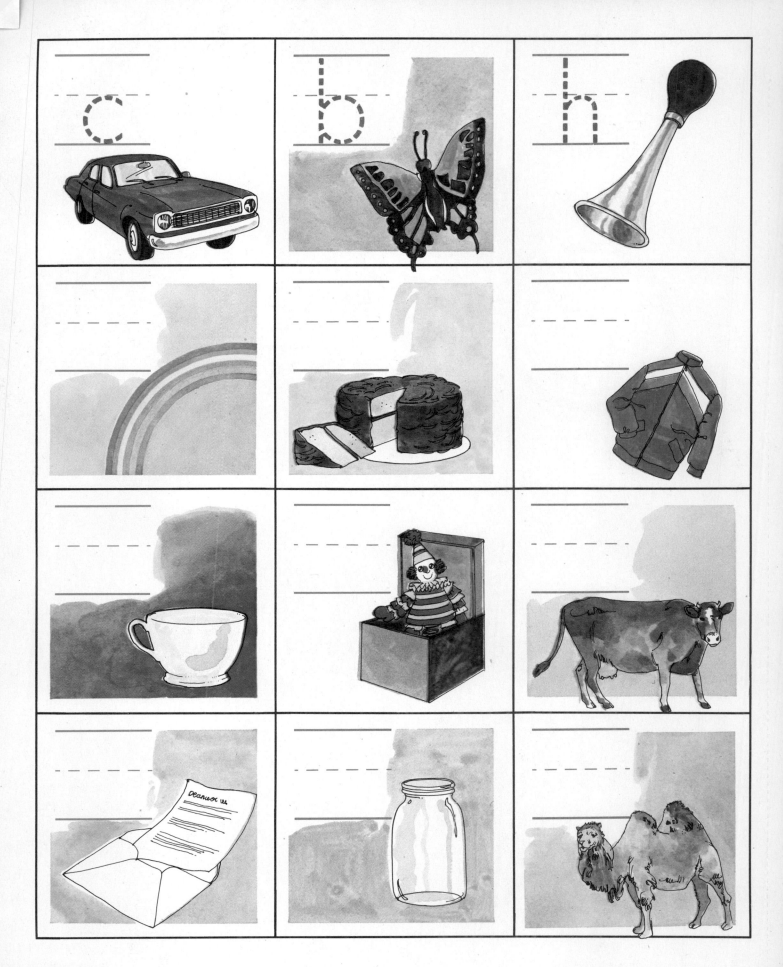

run

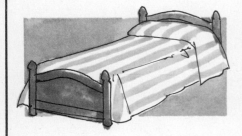 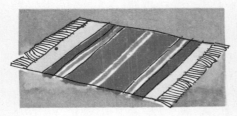 

r<u>u</u>n

run   r_n

bun   b_n

sun   s_n

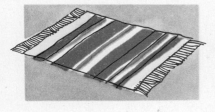
r<u>a</u>g
r<u>u</u>g

n<u>u</u>t
n<u>e</u>t

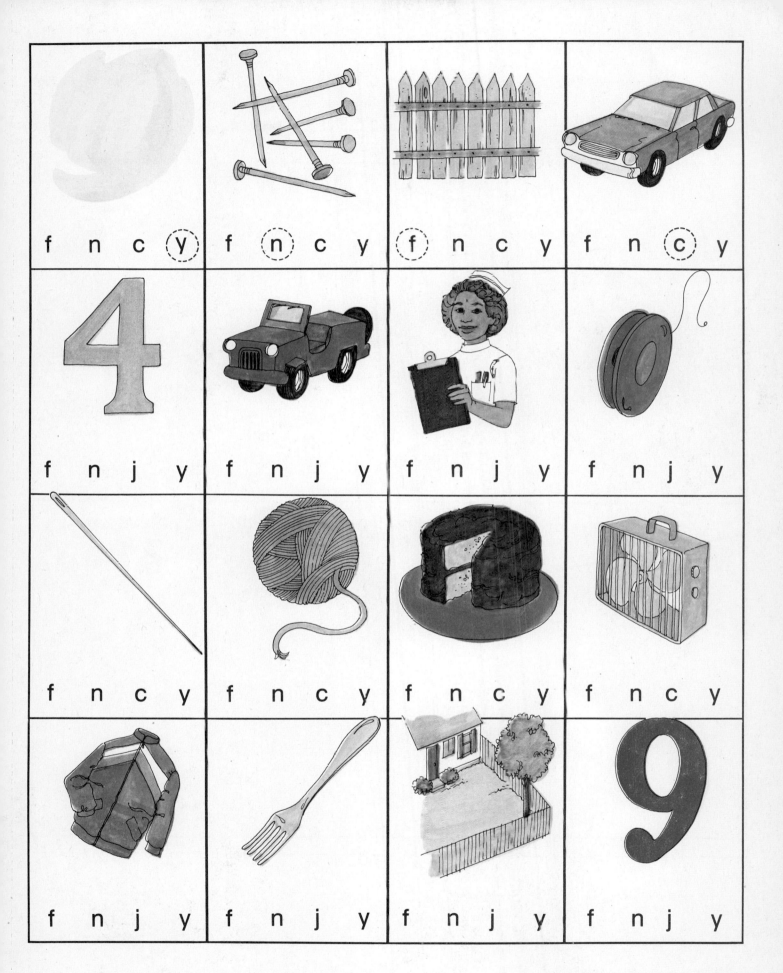

f n c (y)	f (n) c y	(f) n c y	f n (c) y
f n j y	f n j y	f n j y	f n j y
f n c y	f n c y	f n c y	f n c y
f n j y	f n j y	f n j y	f n j y

Can Jill and Bill run?

Yes.

Can Lad run?

No.

Can Lad ride this?

yes   no

Can Lad hide this?

yes   no

Can I ride this?

yes   no

Can I ride this?

yes   no

I s   I s   I s

Is this Lad?

This is Lad.

is   is   — —

Rosa rides.

This is Rosa.

This is Jill.

Jill hides.

Jill can ride.

This is Jill.

Lad rides this.

Rosa hides this.

Rosa and Lad go.

Bill is here.

Jill is here.

Rosa is here.

here _ere ____

Rosa hides.

Rosa is here.

Rosa rides.

Lad is here.

Lad rides.

Lad runs.

Is Bill here? _____ yes | no

Is Jill here? _____ yes | no

Is Lad here? _____ yes | no

Bill is not here.

Jill is not here.

Rosa is not here.

not _ot ___

Is this Bill?

This is Bill.

This is not Bill.

This is Jill.

Is this Jill?

This is Bill.

This is Jill.

This is not Jill.

Is Lad here?

Lad is here.

Lad is not here.

This is Lad.

Is Rosa here?

Rosa is not here.

Rosa is here.

Rosa hides.

This is Jesus.

Jesus is here.

Jesus is here.

Bill is here.

Lad is here.

This is not Jesus.

This is Jesus.

This is Rosa.

Can Jesus ride?

Jesus is not here.

Jesus can not ride.

Jesus can ride.

Is Lad Here?

Here is Jill.

Bill is not here.

Lad is not here.

Here is Bill.

Jill runs . . . and runs.

Bill is here.

And here is Lad.

Lad runs.

And here is Jill.

Is Bill here? _____ yes | no

Is Jill here? _____ yes | no

Can Lad run? _____ yes | no

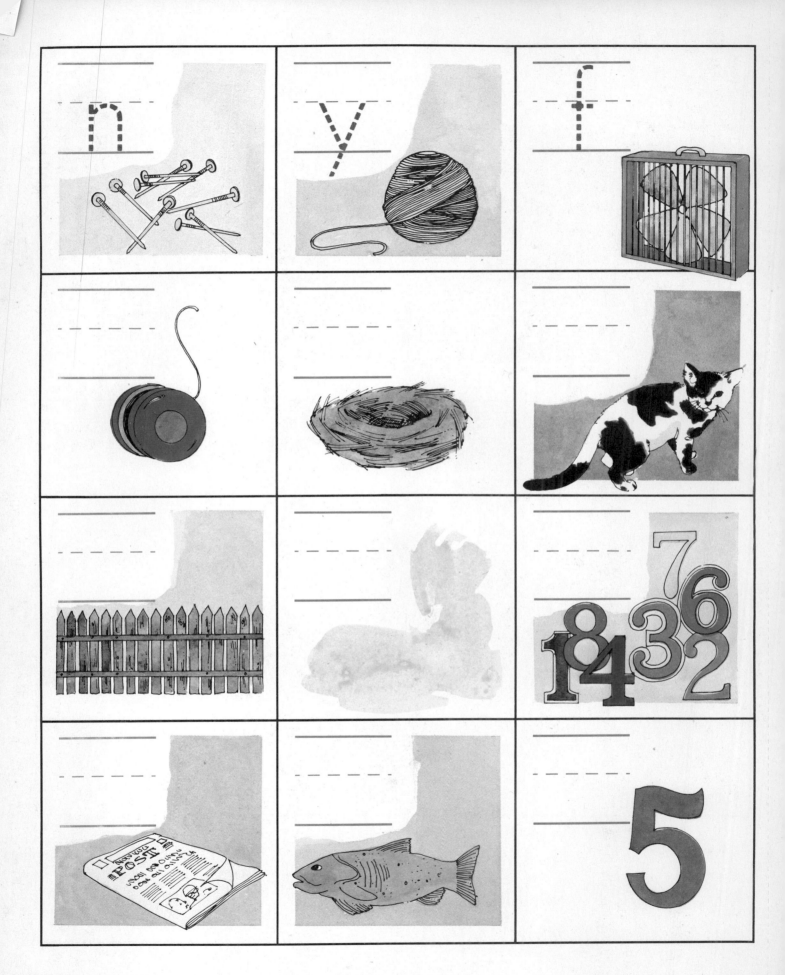

not

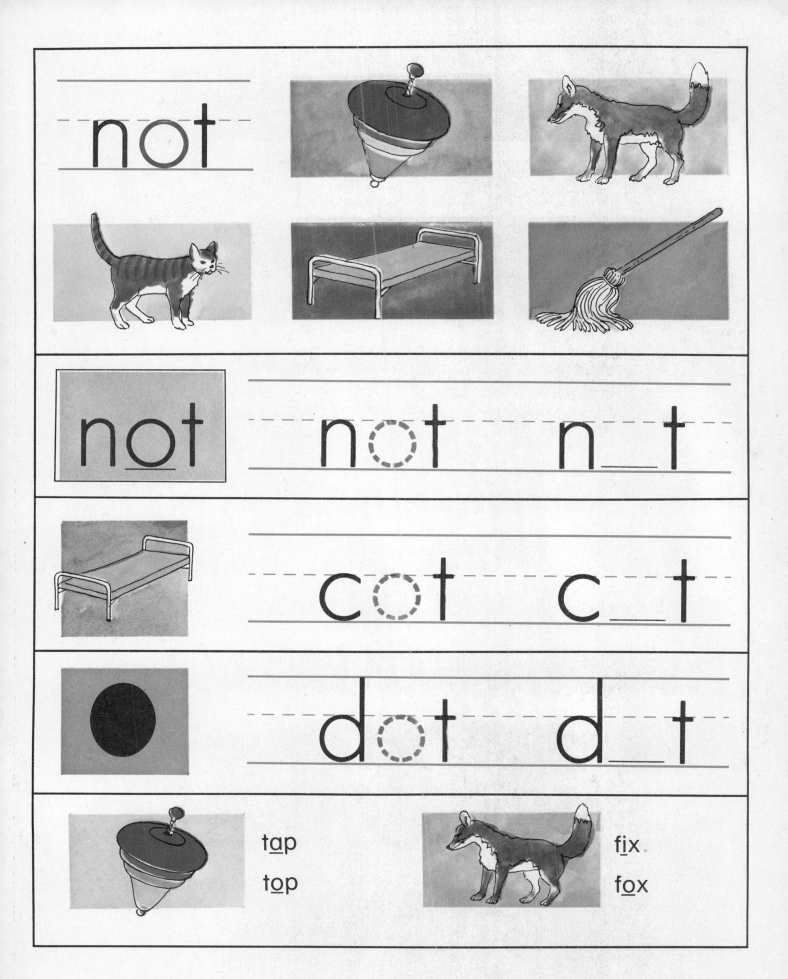

not

not   n__t

cot   c__t

dot   d__t

t<u>a</u>p
t<u>o</u>p

f<u>i</u>x
f<u>o</u>x

t (g) d c   t g (d) c   (t) g d c   t g d (c)

t f d g   t f d g   t f d g   t f d g

n d t g   n d t g   n d t g   n d t g

g t y d   g t y d   g t y d   g t y d

A duck is here.

Here is a duck.

A duck can go.

Is this a duck?

This is a duck.

This is a ride.

A duck is not here.

Is this a duck?

This is a duck.

This is a ride.

This is not a duck.

This is a duck.

Lad can go.

A duck is here.

A duck hides.

Jill hides.

A duck is not here.

Can Lad get a duck?

Lad can not get a duck.

get   _et   ___

Can Bill get this?

Bill can ride this.

Bill can not get this.

Bill can go.

Can Bill and Jill run?

Bill and Jill can hide.

Bill and Jill can not run.

Bill and Jill can run.

Can Jill and Bill get Lad?

Jill and Bill can get Lad.

Jill and Bill can not get Lad.

Jill and Bill can not go.

Ben Ben Ben

This is Ben.

Ben can ride this.

Ben rides here.

Ben _en ___

Ben is here.

Ben is not here.

Lad is here.

Lad is not here.

Ben is not here.

Bill is here.

Lad is not here.

Lad runs.

Bill is here.

Ben is here.

Lad is not here.

Lad runs.

Bill can get this.

Ben can get this.

Lad is here.

Lad is not here.

Ted Ted Ted

Here is Ted.

Ted can run.

Ted can get this.

Ted Ted

Am I Ted? _____ yes | no

Am I Ben? _____ yes | no

Am I Bill? _____ yes | no

Is this Ted? _____ yes | no

Is this Ben? _____ yes | no

Is Ted here? _____ yes | no

Is Ted here? _____ yes | no

Is Jill here? _____ yes | no

Is Ben here? _____ yes | no

Ted hides. _____ yes | no

Rosa rides. _____ yes | no

Ted is here. _____ yes | no

made made made

Jesus made a duck.

Ted made a duck.

made ade

Jesus made this duck.

This duck runs.

This duck hides.

This duck rides.

Ted made this duck.

This duck runs.

This duck can not run.

This duck hides.

Ben made this duck.

This duck can go.

This duck can hide.

This duck can not go.

A Duck

Here, Ben.

Here is a duck.

This duck can get this.

Here, duck.

Here, duck.

Get this.

No!

This duck runs and hides.

Here, duck.

This duck can not get this.

This duck runs.

This duck can get Ted.

This duck can get Bill.

And this duck can get Ben.

Is Ben here? _____ yes | no

Can this duck hide? _____ yes | no

Can this duck get Ben and Ted? __ yes | no

Ben

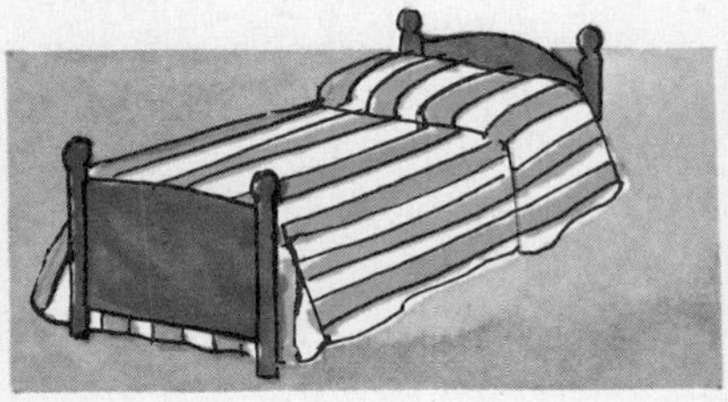

Ben Ben B_n

10 ten t_n

hen h_n

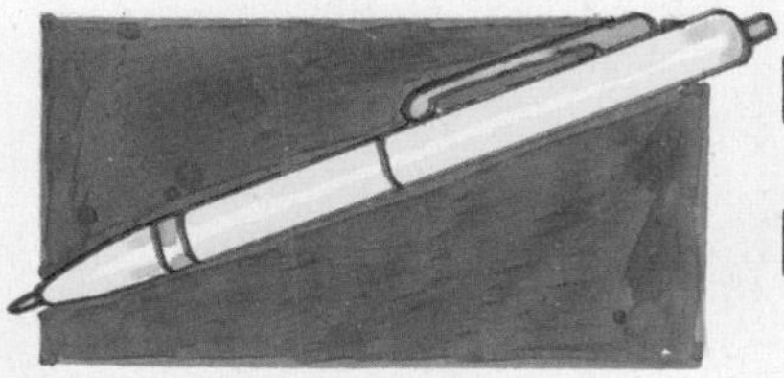

pen   net
pan   not

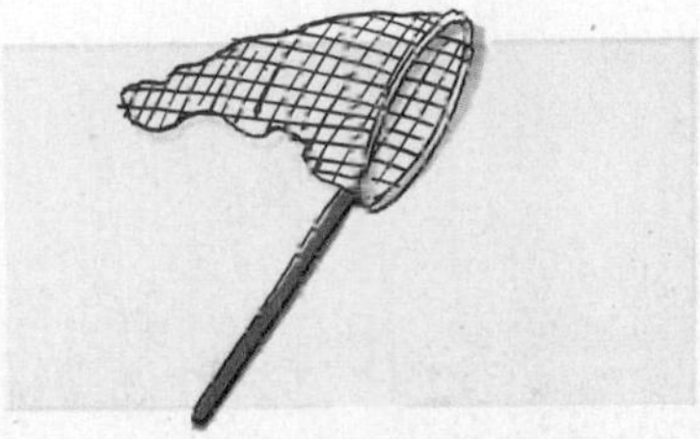

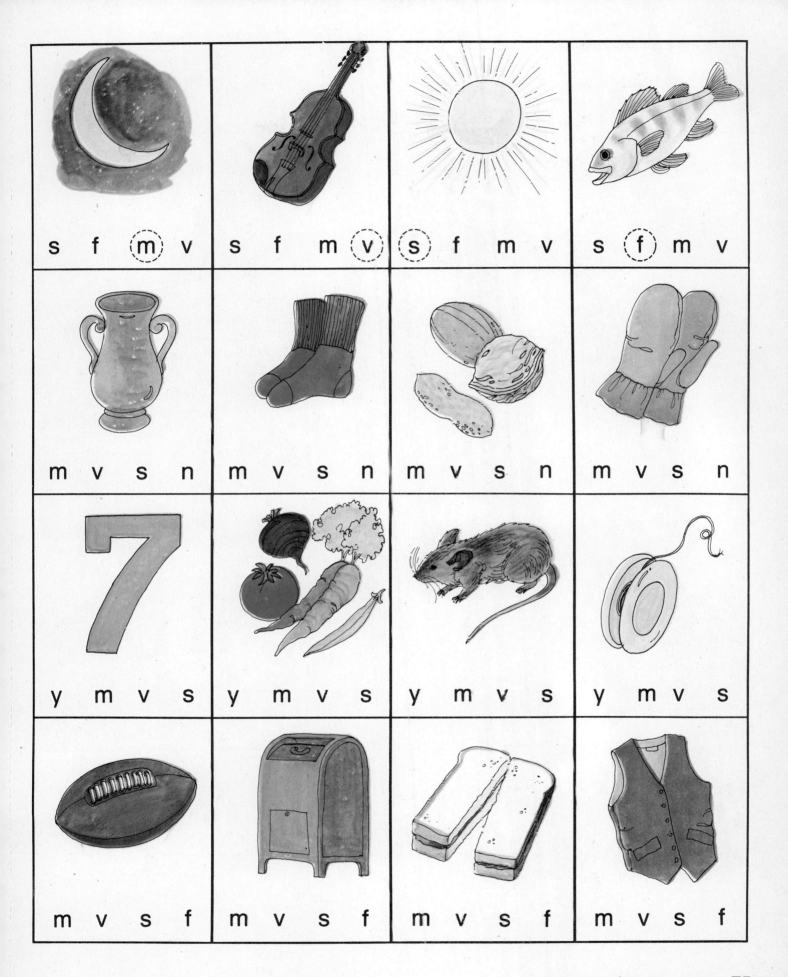

s f (m) v s f m (v) (s) f m v s (f) m v

m v s n m v s n m v s n m v s n

y m v s y m v s y m v s y m v s

m v s f f m v s f f m v s f f m v s f

Here is Nan.

Nan can ride this.

Nan _an __

Is Ben here? _____ yes | no
Can Nan hide here? _ yes | no
Is Jill here? _____ yes | no
Can Lad hide here? _ yes | no

Is this Nan? _____ yes | no
Is this Ted? _____ yes | no
Can Nan hide here? _ yes | no

Is this Nan? _____ yes | no
Is this Rosa? _____ yes | no
Is this Ted? _____ yes | no

Nan, look.

Look at this.

Look at this go, Ted.

look at

Ben and Lad look at a duck.

Ben and Lad hide.

Ben and Lad get a duck.

Ben and Lad look at a duck.

Jill and Rosa look at a duck.

Ben and Lad look at Jill and Rosa.

Rosa and Jill look at Ted.

Nan and Ted run.

Ben and Lad look at a ride.

Nan and Ted look at a ride.

Jesus made this.

Jesus made this.

Jesus made

Jesus made

Ted said, "Ben, look at Rosa."

Rosa said, "Look, Lad. Look here."

Ben said, "Look at Lad go!"

said _aid ___

"Nan, look at this," said Jill.

"Look at Nan hide," said Bill.

"Look at Nan ride," said Ted.

Pet Shop

"A duck is here," said Nan.

"Lad is here," said Nan.

"Jill runs and hides," said Nan.

Nan said, "Can I get a duck here?"

Nan said, "Lad is here."

Nan said, "I can not get a duck here."

DUCKS

Can Nan Go?

Nan said, "Look, Ted."

Ted said, "Go, Nan, go."

"I can go," said Nan.

Ben said, "Lad! Lad!"

Rosa said, "Look at Lad!"

"Nan can not go," said Ted.

Ted said, "Go, Nan, go."

Bill said, "Ben, get Lad."

Rosa said, "Lad can not run."

Jill said, "Nan can go."

Is Bill here? _____ yes | no

Can Nan go? _____ yes | no

Can Lad run? _____ yes | no

Can Lad get Nan? _____ yes | no

J ill

i ll
h m f

i ll
b p f

B en

_ en
b h d

_ en
b d t

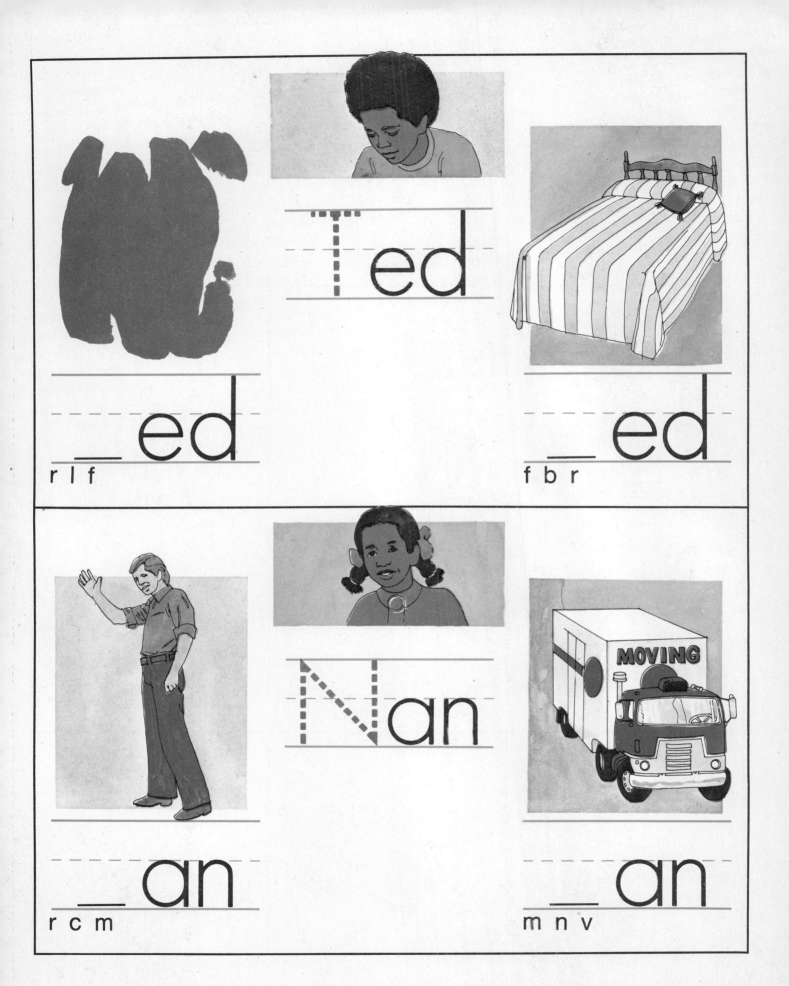

Ted

__ed
r l f

__ed
f b r

Nan

__an
r c m

__an
m n v

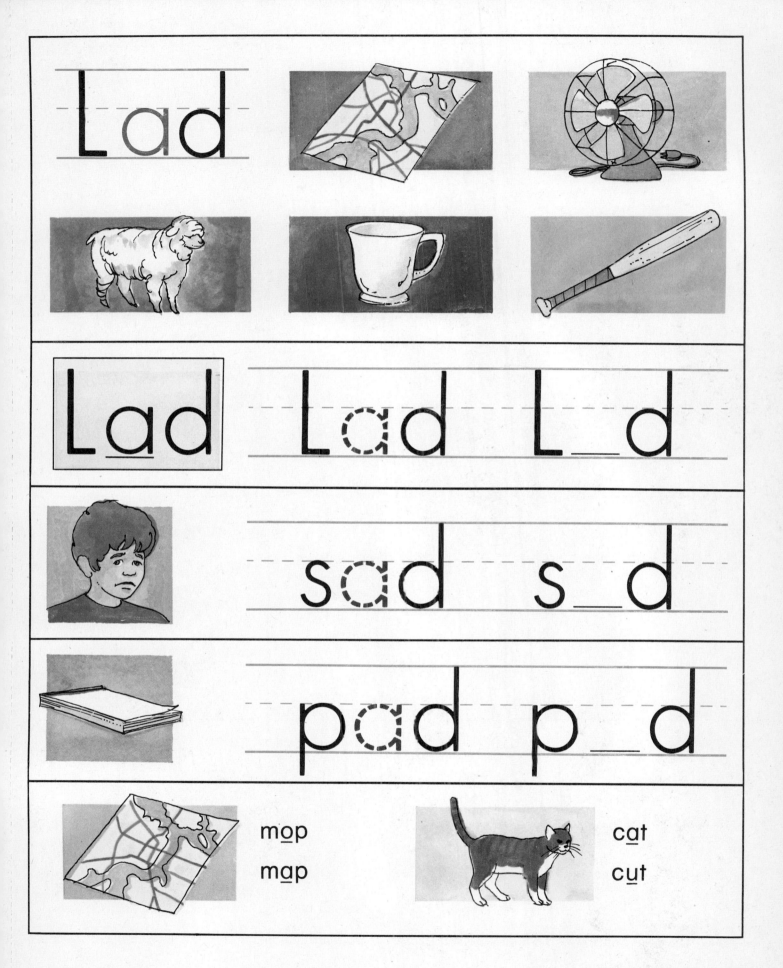

Lad

Lad   Lad   L_d

sad   s_ d

pad   p_ d

mop   cat
map   cut

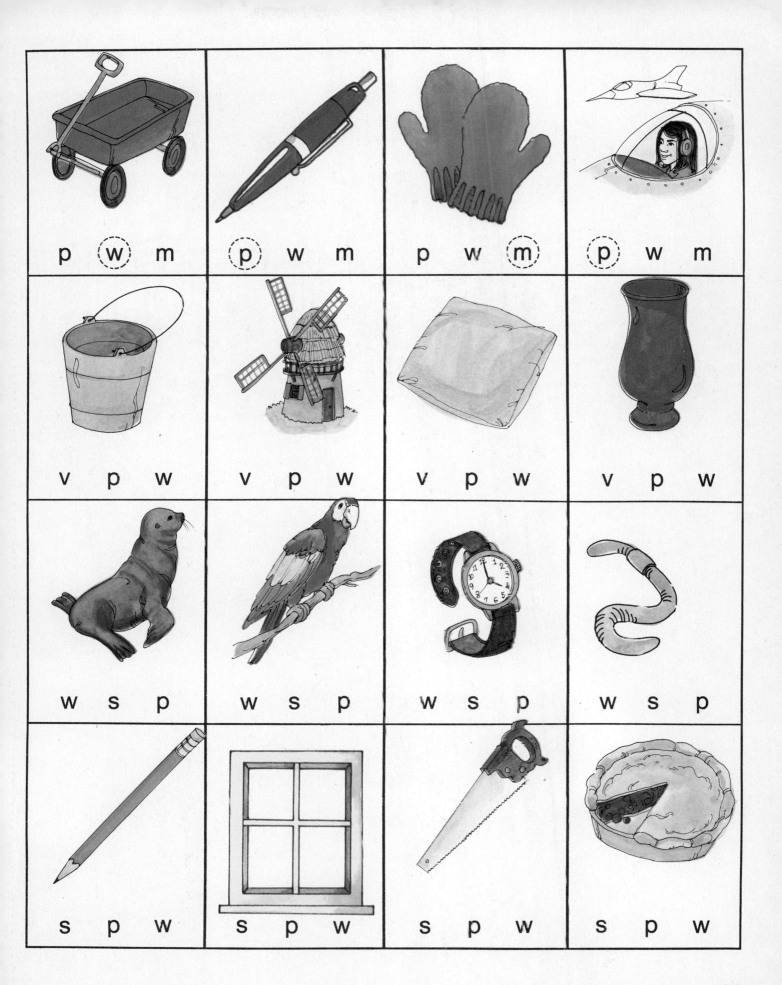

p (w) m   (p) w m   p w (m)   (p) w m

v p w   v p w   v p w   v p w

w s p   w s p   w s p   w s p

s p w   s p w   s p w   s p w

the park the park

This is the park.

Nan and Jill ride at the park.

Ted and Bill ride at the park.

Rosa runs at the park.

the _ ark

Vocabulary: **the park**/Decoding

A duck is at the park.

A duck hides at the park.

Lad is at the park.

Bill, Ted, Nan, and Ben run.

This is not a park.

Lad is at the park.

Rosa said, "I can ride this."

A duck is at the park.

Jill is at the park.

Ben and Nan hide here.

A duck rides at the park.

Bill and Ted ride at the park.

Jill said, "I will hide here."

Rosa said, "I will hide here."

"I will run and hide," said Ted.

Will Lad run and get this?

Lad will not run and get this.

Lad will run and get this.

Lad rides at the park.

Will Rosa get Nan?

Rosa will get Nan.

Nan will get Rosa.

Rosa will not get Ted.

Will Lad get the duck?

Lad will not get the duck.

Lad will get the duck.

Lad will run and hide.

like to

like to

"Jill and I like to ride at the park," said Nan.

"Lad and I like to run here," said Ben.

"Ted and I like to go to the park," said Bill.

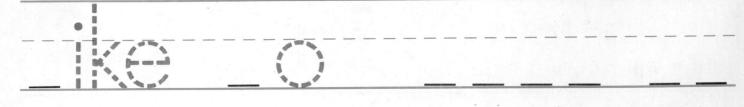

"I like to ride this," said Nan.

"I will run," said Nan.

"I will hide here," said Nan.

Rosa said, "I will not like this."

Rosa said, "I like to ride here."

Rosa said, "I like this."

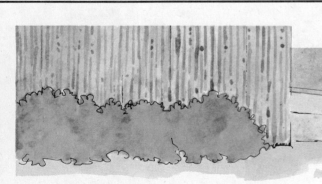

Ted and Bill will hide.

Ted and Bill like to run.

Ted and Bill ride here.

Nan and Ted

Nan and Ted like to go to the park.

Ted and Nan like the rides at the park.

Will Ted and Nan go to the park?

Here is Nan.

Nan is at the park.

Will Ted go to the park?

Yes, Ted is at the park.

Look at Ted go.

Will Bill and Jill go to the park?

Bill and Jill look at Nan and Ted.

Bill and Jill like the park.

Bill and Jill run to Nan and Ted.

Will Bill, Jill, Nan, and Ted ride?

Is Lad at the park? _____ yes | no

Will Bill and Jill go to the park? _____ yes | no

Will Nan and Ted go to the park? ___ yes | no

Is Ben at the park? _____ yes | no

like   bike   hike

I can ride a _____.

look   book   cook

Ted and Bill _____.

park dark mark

The park is ____.

run sun fun

This is ___.

| Bill | run | not | Lad | Ben |

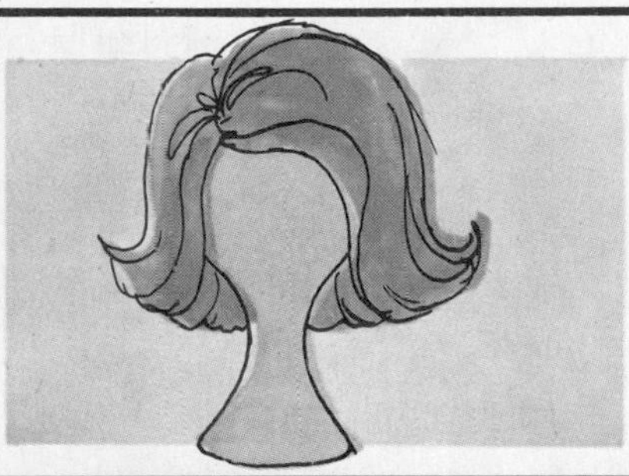

wig
w<u>a</u>g

w<u>i</u>g

p<u>o</u>t
p<u>e</u>t

p_t

t<u>a</u>p
t<u>o</u>p

t_p

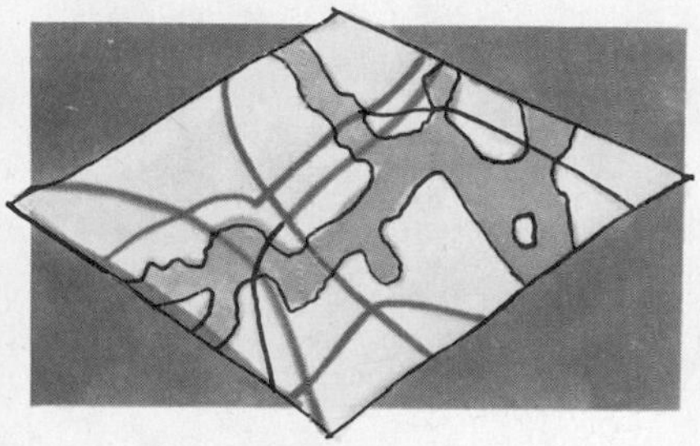

m<u>a</u>p
m<u>o</u>p

m_p

n<u>u</u>t
n<u>e</u>t

n_t

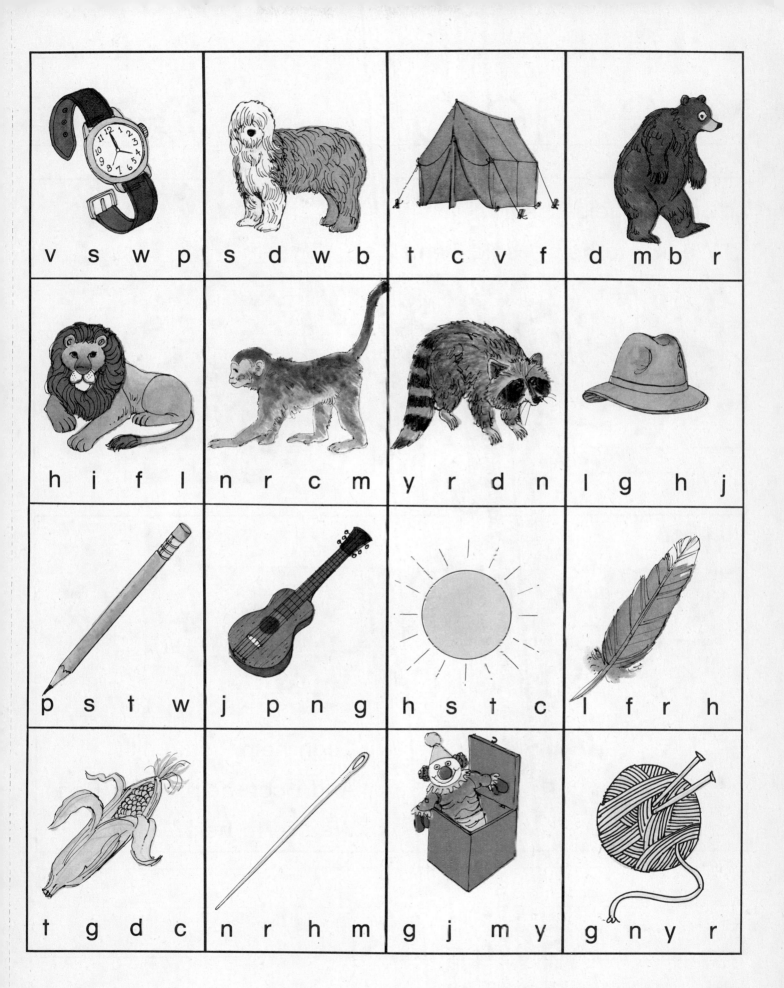

v s **w** p	s d w b	t c v f	d m **b** r
h i f l	n r c m	y r d n	l g h j
p s t w	j p n g	h s t c	l f r h
t g d c	n r h m	g j m y	g n y r

we help

we help

"Can we help?" said Jill.

"We like to help," said Ben.

"I can help," said Jill.

"And I can help," said Ben.

"We like to help."

We can go help.

We can not help.

We run and hide.

We like to help.

We can not help.

We hide here.

We will not help Ben.

We will help Ben.

We will hide.

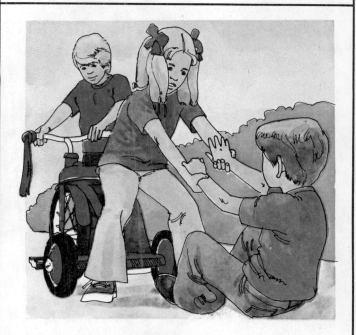

We can help Ben.

We can not help Ben.

Ben hides here.

are　are　are

Here are Ted and Bill.

Ted and Bill are at the park.

Rosa and Nan are here.

Jill and Lad are here.

are　are　＿＿＿

Are Bill and Ted here?

Nan and Ben are here.

Bill and Ted are here.

Ted and Ben are here.

Are Nan and Ted here?

Nan and Ted are here.

Nan and Ted are not here.

Nan and Bill are at the park.

Can Nan help Lad?

Nan can help Lad.

Nan and Ted are here.

Nan is not here.

Bill said, "Ben, stop."

"Stop and look," said Bill.

stop stop ____

"Can we stop here?" said Rosa.

"We can help here," said Nan.

"We can stop here," said Nan.

"We can ride here," said Nan.

Will Lad run?

Lad will hide.

Lad will stop.

Lad will run to Ben.

Will Lad stop?

The duck will stop.

Lad will run.

Lad will stop here.

At the Park

Nan and Jill are at the park.

Rosa is at the park.

Bill and Ted look at Nan, Jill, and Rosa.

Bill and Ted run to the park.

Here are Rosa and Ted.

Rosa and Ted like the park.

Look at Rosa go.

Ted runs to a ride.

Ben and Lad run to the park.

Here are Bill and Ben.

Ben and Bill can not go.

Ben and Bill can not ride this.

Ted can help Bill.

Bill and Ted can go.

Bill and Ted can ride this.

Are Nan and Jill at the park? __ yes | no

Can Ted and Ben ride? _____ yes | no

Can Bill and Ted ride? _____ yes | no

w v p d

j b l g

m d s b

v t g l

s c v f

r m g j

y p w g

r c m h

d l h g

l c r n

w m f t

f r c b

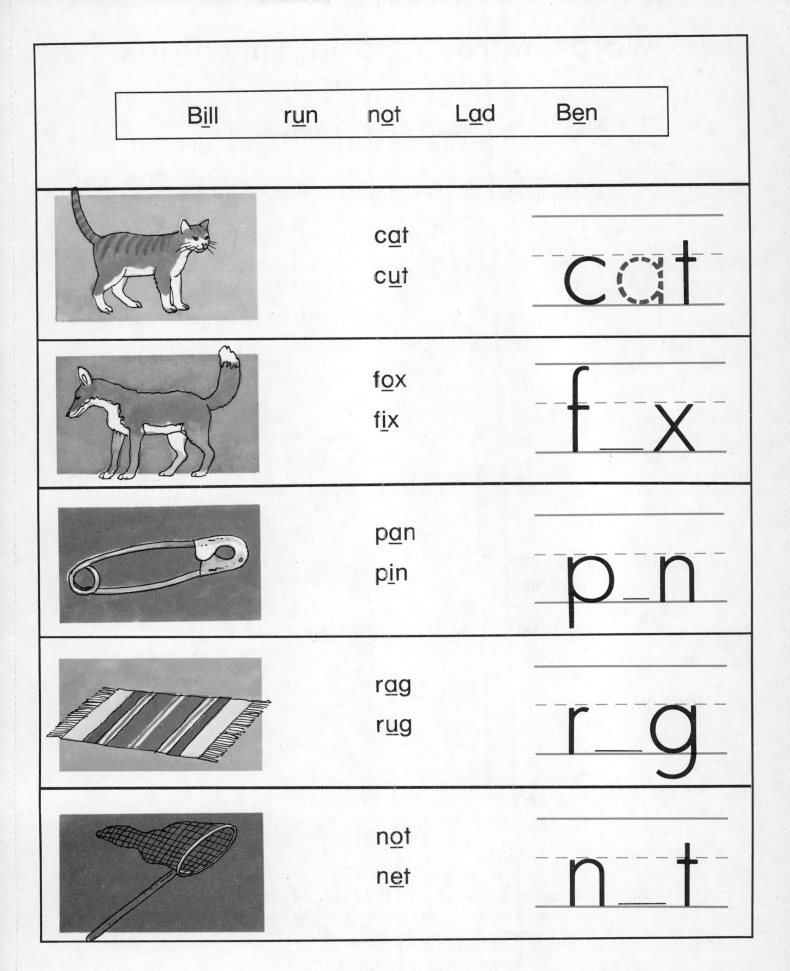

cat
cut

c a t

fox
fix

f _ x

pan
pin

p _ n

rag
rug

r _ g

not
net

n _ t

Words Introduced in This Book

A Time to Play introduces 41 words. These words are reinforced through a carefully sequenced word analysis program. This basic vocabulary prepares the child for reading *Seek and Find,* Level Three.

Illustrations by Charles Molina and Pat Morrison